ELLi
A Day IN the Life of A Kid with ADHD

ARi H.G. Yates

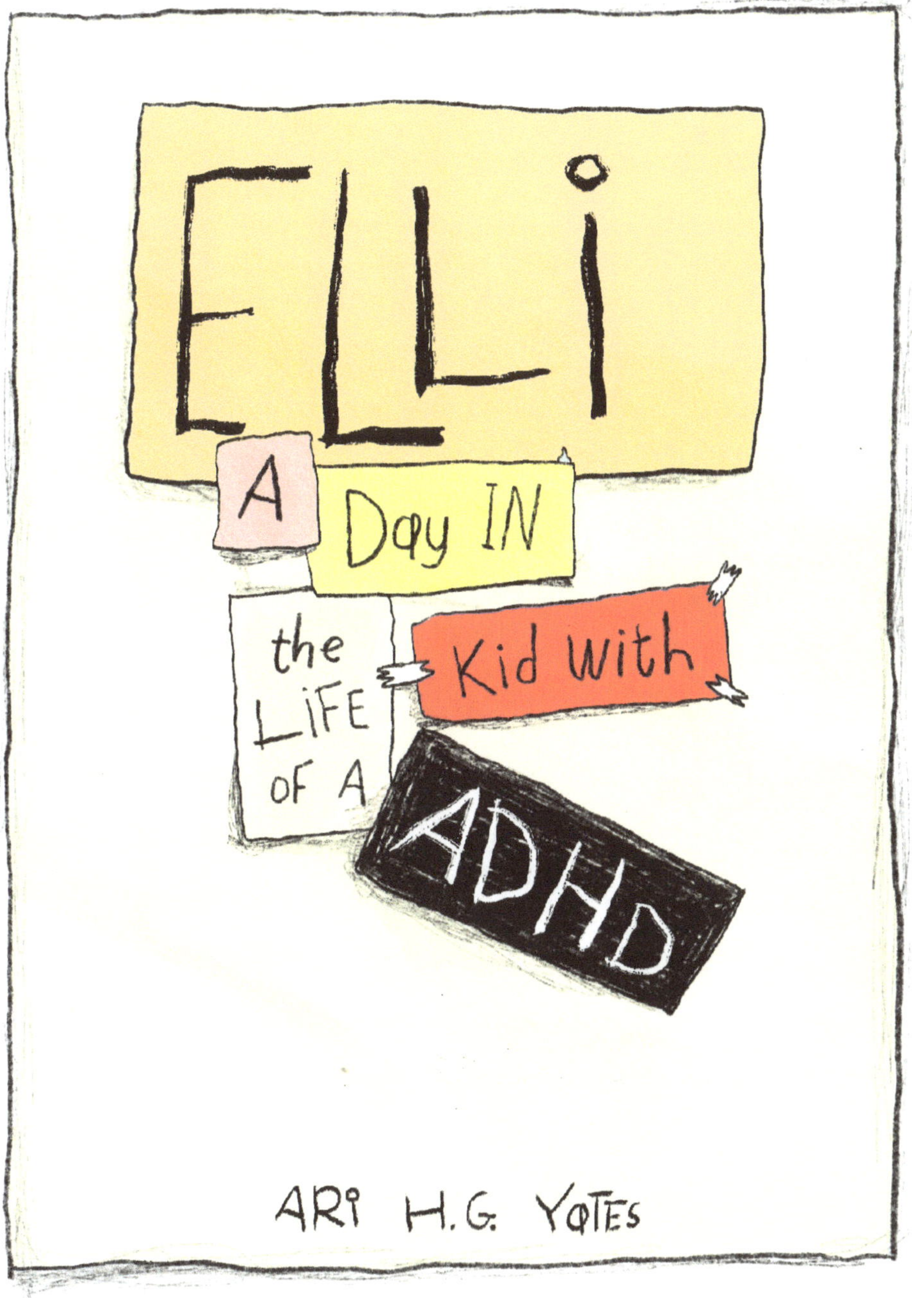

(you can doodle here)

THIS BOOK BELONGS TO...

This book is dedicated to my father, who passed while I was writing it.
—Ari Hlynur Guðmundsson Yates

Elli, A Day in the Life of a Kid with ADHD
Ari Hlynur Guðmundsson Yates

Copyright © 2022 CAST, Inc. and David Berman Communications. All rights reserved.

No part of this publication may be reproduced or transmitted in any form or by any means, electronic or mechanical, including photocopy, recording, or any information storage and retrieval systems, without permission in writing from the publisher.

Paperback ISBN 978-1-930583-90-0 (paper)
Ebook ISBN 978-1-930583-91-7 (EPUB)

Author: Ari Hlynur Guðmundson Yates
Illustrations: Ari H.G. Yates and Elias Bjarnar Baldurssen
Assistant Illustrator: Lea My Ib
Language Adaptation: Anna H. Yates
Design and Typography: Ari H.G. Yates and David Berman
Proofreading: Ray Farmilo
Story Editor: David Berman

Originally published in Icelandic

Additional design and production by Happenstance Type-O-Rama

Publisher: David Berman Communications

A note about the typeface
This book uses Lexend Deca, a font designed for all readers by Bonnie Shaver-Troup, EdD. Available in Google Fonts. Visit lexend.com to learn the full story behind this accessible font selection.

Learn more about author Ari H.G. Yates at www.teiknari.com

For David Berman Communications, visit www.davidberman.com

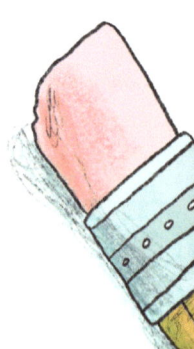

About this book
—*From the author*

This book was written in 2014, based on interviews with Elías (Elli), a 9-year-old boy with ADHD. Elías is the son of my good friend Sigríður. I interviewed Elli and then combined a few stories into one story—which became this book.

Elli is a talented illustrator and so I got the idea to let him illustrate the book with me. Everything that the character "Elli" draws in the story—as well as everything he is imagining—Elías (Elli) actually illustrated in real life. One of the main goals of the book was to inspire children with ADHD: "If Elli can draw such beautiful pictures in a *real* book, maybe I can too." After finishing writing the book, I discovered that I too have ADHD, and I have used that knowledge to get most of my symptoms (which had impacted my life in a serious way) under control. For that I am very grateful.

Children with ADHD often feel misunderstood and get negative feedback when they have trouble following instructions, staying still, and maintaining focus on projects that do not interest them. Although I think it's important not to gloss over these negative aspects, the main focus of the book is that it's possible to approach ADHD in a positive way. With the right tools in hand, you can harness your ADHD into a kind of a superpower!

My hope is that children with ADHD can see themselves in Elli when they read his story and realize they are not alone. The book also takes a look at the (often) complicated relationship between parents and their children. Parents also make mistakes and can also feel shame—they also need time to learn. Sigríður Ása, Elli's mom, told me that through taking part in this project, she managed to understand and appreciate her son better. One could not hope for any more than that.

Even though the subject matter is indeed a serious one, it's important to me that it's fun and uplifting. I approach everything with a dash of humour and in my experience it not only helps us enjoy life more, but actually helps with problem-solving—even if the problem in question is a serious one.

You can't expect to cover a subject in its entirety in one book (no matter how awesome it is). However, I hope that I managed to cover it well enough in these pages to be of help (and enjoyment) to the reader.

> ...*if you are still reading this and you have ADHD, congratulations are in order. WELL DONE, YOU!!!*

—Ari H. G. Yates

ELLi

A Day in the Life of a Kid with ADHD

~~Ari H.C. Yates~~
—Elli

Hi! My name is Elli!

I'm 9 years old and I have ADHD.

That means I sometimes do things without thinking of the consequences.

I find it hard to concentrate...except when I really like what I'm doing. Then I concentrate REALLY WELL.

When there's lots of noise around me, I sometimes act up...or make my own weird noises!

Sometimes my teacher gets angry with me and says I'm naughty. But I don't mean to be. Sometimes I just can't help it!

I study best when everything's quiet around me.

I'm good at math and reading, but I love art best of all.

All my classmates say I'm the best at school in drawing. They all want to see my artwork!

I like being outside at recess. I'm good at pretty much every sport I've tried: my favorite is soccer.

I'm really good at skateboarding too. I can do all sorts of stunts that only the big kids can do.

One day I was on my way to school, when I suddenly spotted a SWORD! It was sticking out from under a pile of leaves.

Sword!

I had to take a closer look.

The dinosaur had almost swallowed me up but luckily I was victorious!

I started wondering:
"What would it be like to be an actual astronaut?"

"How do you sleep out in space?"

"What do you have for dinner?"

"What if you need to poop?"

In my next class, my math teacher gave me my very own separate desk: it helps me concentrate better.

I finished all my arithmetic, and my teacher gave me a star!

I took my star with me to art class: it's my favorite class so I love going there.

Art is no problem at all.

I just draw and color whatever I like. Nobody gets upset with me in art class.

My art teacher said: "That is a great picture you made, Elli."

And he hung it up high so my classmates could see it.

After school, it was my friend Daniel's birthday. He had invited the entire class to a costume party.

I decided to dress up as a scary skeleton!

I got dressed really quickly. Mom was busy doing something else.

When I got to the party, everyone was playing.

"Be good, sweetheart," said Mom.

We said goodbye, and I ran to Daniel.

We played tag, superheroes, cowboys and monsters, and cops and robbers.

And we had pizza and cake!

Dad didn't seem to understand that I couldn't leave in the middle of the game.

Mom and Dad were NOT happy with me on the way home.

They told me I had behaved badly at the party,
and Dad had hurt himself trying to catch me.

When everyone had calmed down a bit, we all had a little talk.

"You shouldn't run away from your father when he comes to pick you up," Mom said.

"I'm sorry, Dad," I said. "I didn't mean to be bad. Sometimes I get so excited that I lose control."

"I know, kiddo," Dad replied. "But you must be more careful to listen when you're being picked up. Otherwise we won't be able to let you go to these kinds of parties.",

"I'll try my best," I said.

After a bit of silence my dad added: "You know, Elli, I sometimes lose control too. I didn't mean to get so angry with you earlier. I lost control of my temper when you didn't listen. I shouldn't have done that. I'm very sorry about that, kiddo; I'll try to do better."

"It's OK, Dad," I said. "Maybe we can help each other remember to always be good to one another."

"You know, I think you are absolutely right about that, Elli," Dad answered, smiling.

When I was in bed I told Mom and Dad about everything that had happened that day.

The dinosaur battle, everything I learned about space...

...the star I got for finishing my math assignment and everything that happened at the birthday party.

"Good night, sweetie," Mom and Dad said. "Sweet dreams."

"I'm not sure I can ever fall asleep after such an exciting day," I thought to myself.

"But actually I do need to be well rested for tomorrow; I suspect a certain dinosaur might show up for a rematch!"

www.ingramcontent.com/pod-product-compliance
Lightning Source LLC
Chambersburg PA
CBHW050751110526
44592CB00002B/34